CLEAR LAKE
GIANT BOOK OF FUN

boutique

MARINA

GAS

200 PAGES
Coloring, Games,
Journal Pages,
and special
Clear Lake
memories!

FUN FOR THE WHOLE FAMILY!

CLEAR LAKE

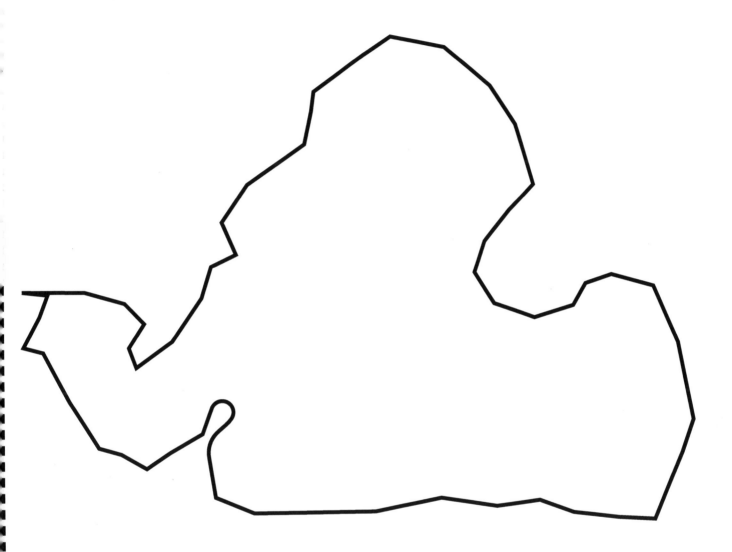

STEUBEN COUNTY, INDIANA

COLORED BY:

DATE:

MY CLEAR LAKE MEMORIES

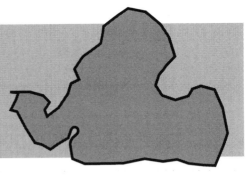

WRITTEN BY:

DATE:

SWIM

COLORED BY:

DATE:

FILL IN THE BLANK SILLY STORY

WATER SPORTS ON CLEAR LAKE

One _____ afternoon, my friends _____,
   adjective   friend's name

_____, and I were riding in our _____ on
friend's name   noun

Clear Lake. The weather forecast called for _____
                                              plural noun

with a high of _____ degrees. The water was
                   number

a refreshing temperature of _____. My friends
                              number

and I decided to try a new water sport. We pulled a

_____ behind our boat and rode on it by
   noun

holding on with our _____. It was so much
                      body part -plural

fun, everyone started to join in and we named our

new water sport _____.
                    noun

Clear Lake memories are the best! I like to write

about them in my diary _____ times a day.
                          number

PLAYED BY:

DATE:

Tic Tac Turtle

PLAYED BY:

DATE:

Water Drops and Boxes

Take turns connecting two water drops (dots). If your line completes a box, write your initials in the box. The person with the most boxes at the end of the game wins!

PLAYED BY:

DATE:

MY CLEAR LAKE MEMORIES

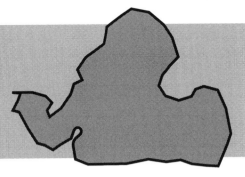

WRITTEN BY:

DATE:

COLORED BY:

DATE:

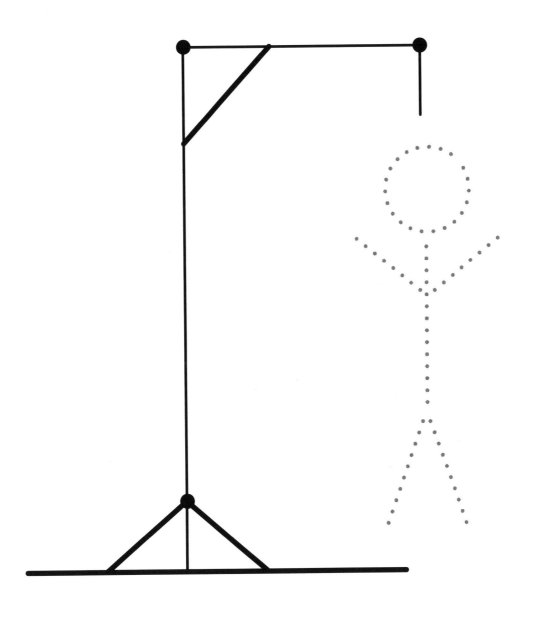

A B C D E F G H I J K L M N

O P Q R S T U V W X Y Z

PLAYED BY:

DATE:

ICE
CREAM

COLORED BY:

DATE:

BOAT PARADE

COLORED BY:

DATE:

FOUR BUOYS IN A ROW

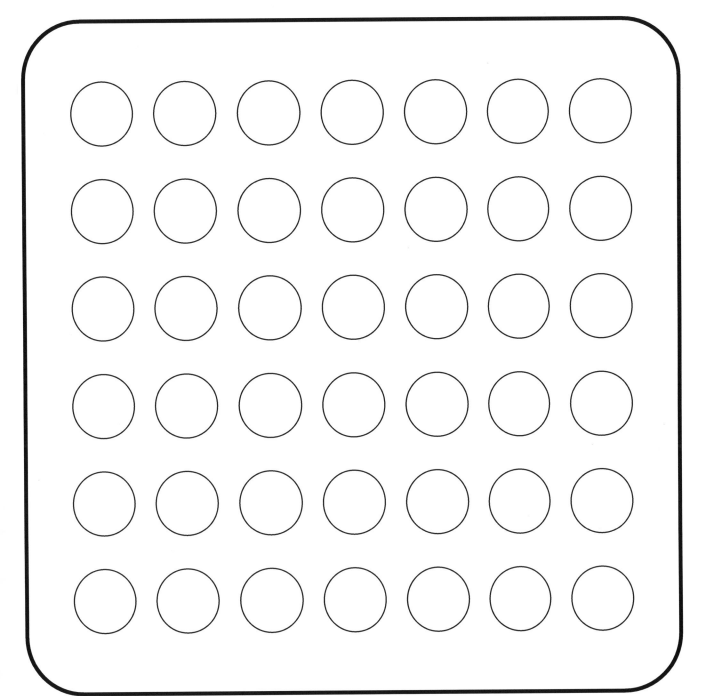

TAKE TURNS COLORING IN THE BUOYS AND
SEE WHO CAN GET FOUR IN A ROW FIRST!
(VERTICAL, HORIZONTAL, OR DIAGONAL)

PLAYED BY:

DATE:

Water Drops and Boxes

Take turns connecting two water drops (dots). If your line completes a box, write your initials in the box. The person with the most boxes at the end of the game wins!

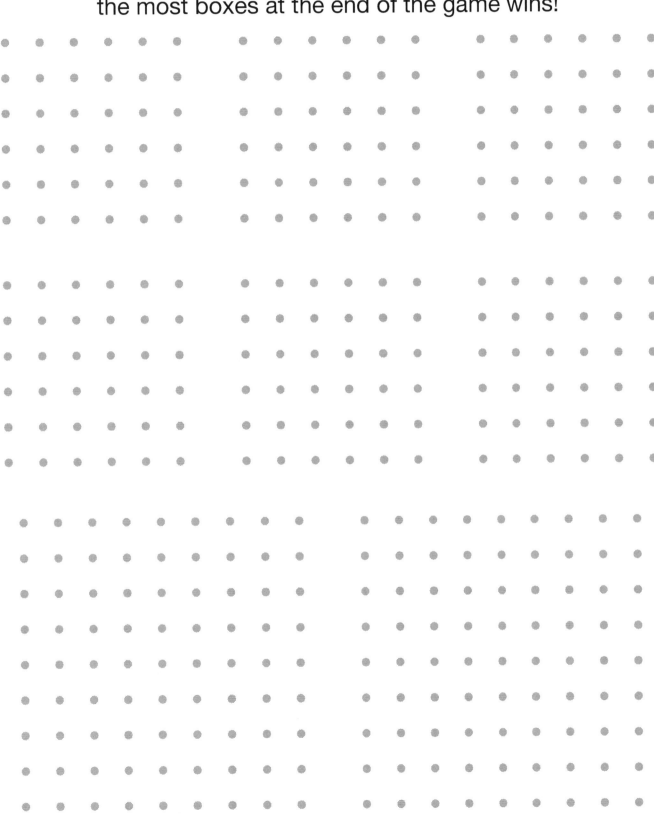

PLAYED BY:

DATE:

Tic Tac Turtle

PLAYED BY:

DATE:

MY CLEAR LAKE MEMORIES

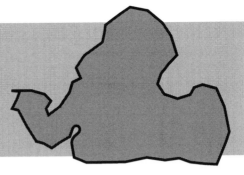

WRITTEN BY:

DATE:

COLORED BY:

DATE:

FLOAT

COLORED BY:

DATE:

COLORED BY:

DATE:

FILL IN THE BLANK SILLY STORY

A CLEAR LAKE EVENING

After a long day of _____ behind our
verb ending in -ing

boat on Clear Lake, it was time to take a break for

dinner. _____ was grilling _____
friend's name   noun

and it smelled _____. As the sun set,
adjective

we decided to all gather around the fire and roast

_____ while we sang
food

_____. What a _____
name of song   adjective

sound! The bugs were biting our

_____ and so _____
body part -plural   friend's name

found the bug spray made by _____
brand name

with the slogan, _____.
slogan

We will always remember this _____
adjective

day at Clear Lake!

PLAYED BY:

DATE:

COLORED BY:

DATE:

PLAYED BY:

DATE:

BOAT

PARADE

COLORED BY:

DATE:

COLORED BY:

DATE:

FOUR BUOYS IN A ROW

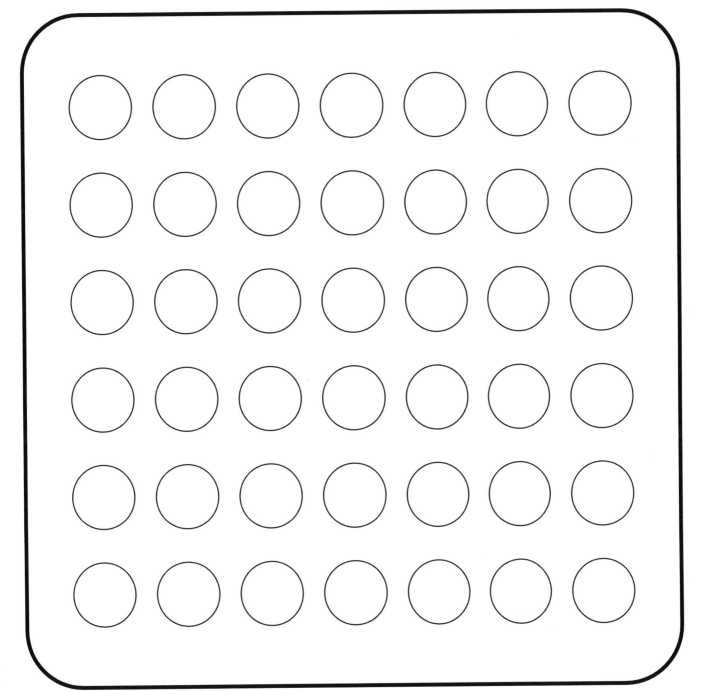

TAKE TURNS COLORING IN THE BUOYS AND
SEE WHO CAN GET FOUR IN A ROW FIRST!
(VERTICAL, HORIZONTAL, OR DIAGONAL)

PLAYED BY:

DATE:

KNEEBOARDING

COLORED BY:

DATE:

MY CLEAR LAKE MEMORIES

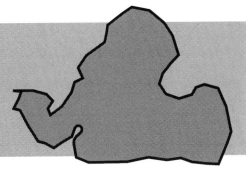

WRITTEN BY:

DATE:

COLORED BY:

DATE:

TUBING

COLORED BY:

DATE:

COLORED BY:

DATE:

Water Drops and Boxes

Take turns connecting two water drops (dots). If your line completes a box, write your initials in the box. The person with the most boxes at the end of the game wins!

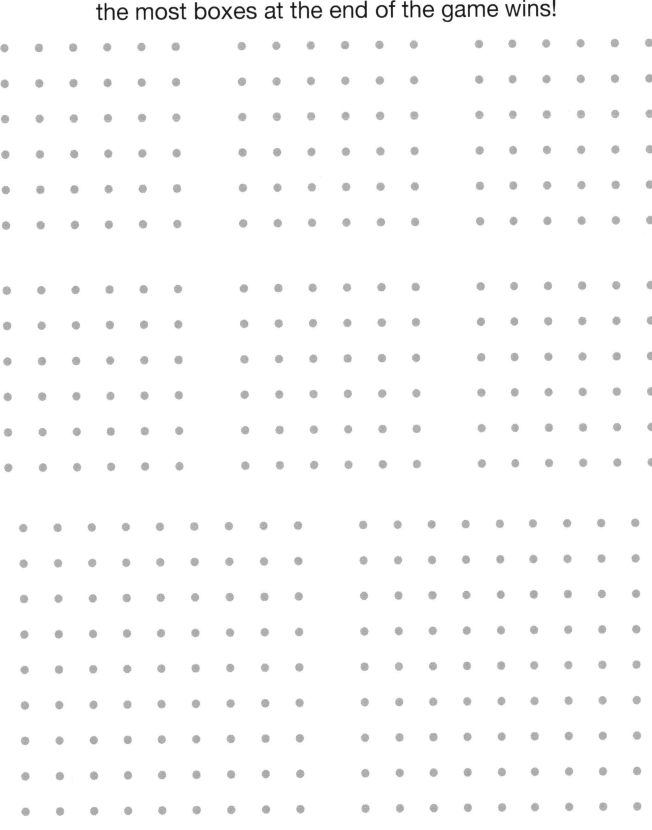

PLAYED BY:

DATE:

BOAT PARADE

COLORED BY:

DATE:

FOUR BUOYS IN A ROW

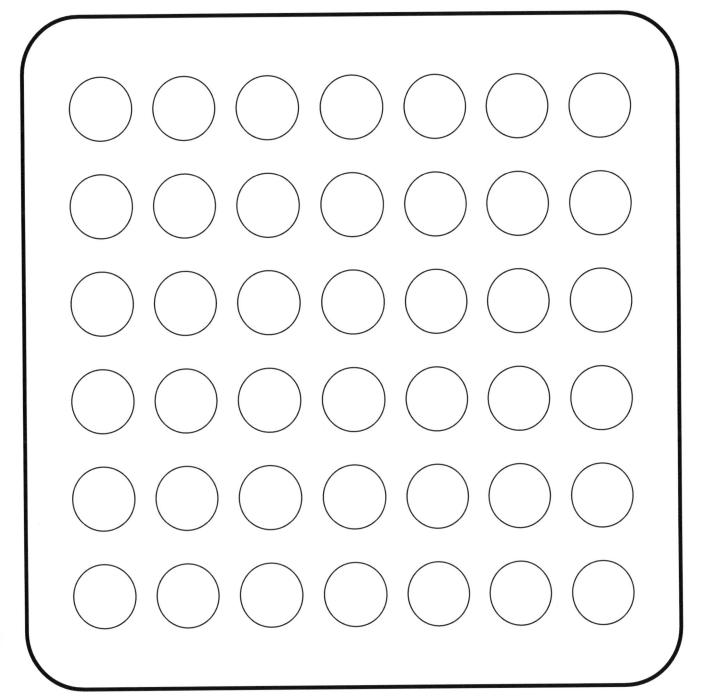

TAKE TURNS COLORING IN THE BUOYS AND
SEE WHO CAN GET FOUR IN A ROW FIRST!
(VERTICAL, HORIZONTAL, OR DIAGONAL)

PLAYED BY:

DATE:

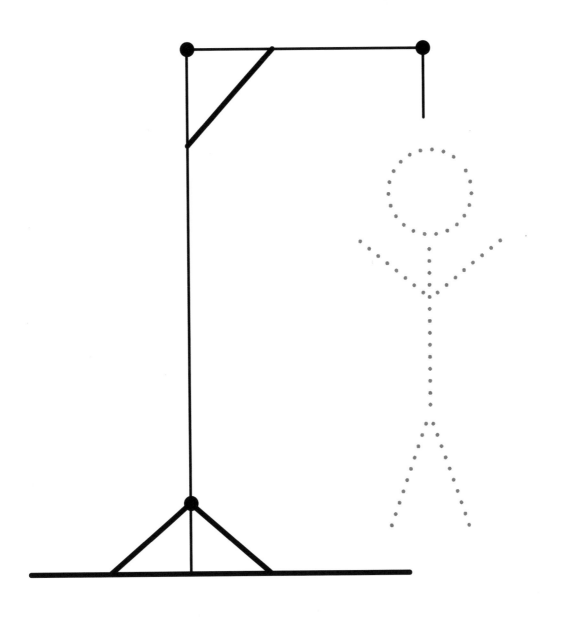

A B C D E F G H I J K L M N
O P Q R S T U V W X Y Z

PLAYED BY:

DATE:

FILL IN THE BLANK SILLY STORY

THE CLEAR LAKE BOAT PARADE

Some years, near Independence Day, Clear Lake

hosts a boat parade. This year, the theme is

_____. We plan to decorate
                party theme

our boat with _____ and _____.
                plural noun   plural noun

_____ is going to drive the boat while
family member's name

_____ and _____ stand
       friend's name   friend's name

in the boat _____. I sure do hope
                   verb ending in -ing

we win! This year the prize for 1st place is a

_____, and the worst boat gets
            noun

_____ dollars.
            number

What a _____ way to celebrate the
               adjective

Fourth of July!

PLAYED BY:

DATE:

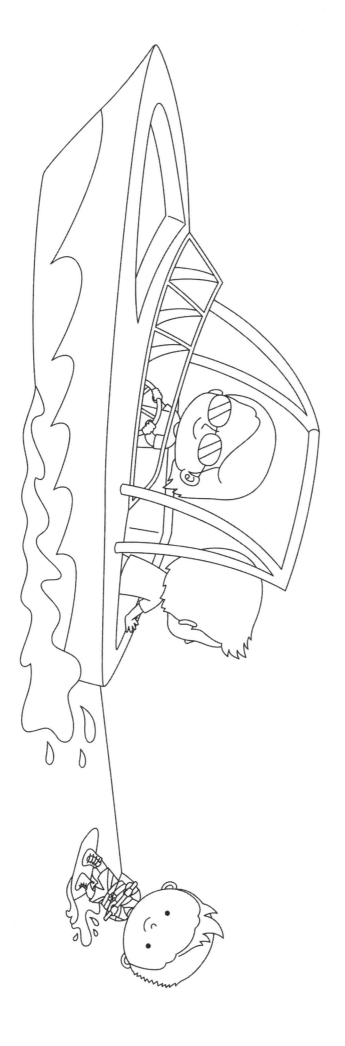

WAKEBOARDING

COLORED BY:

DATE:

KNEEBOARDING

COLORED BY:

DATE:

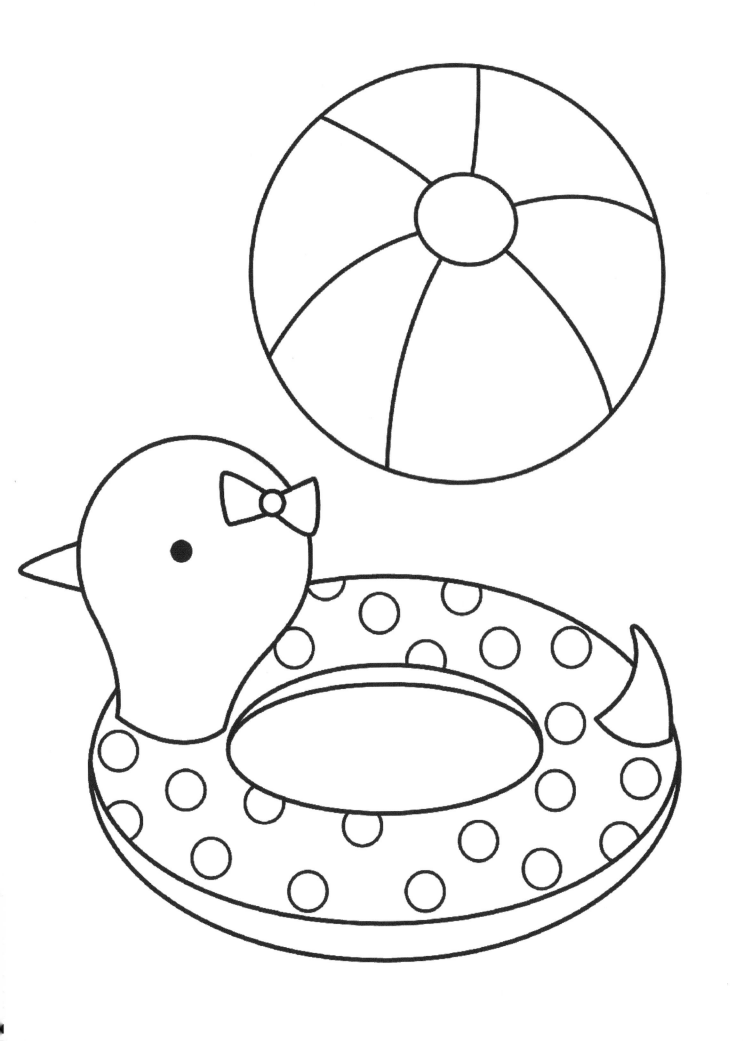

COLORED BY:

DATE:

BAKING

COLORED BY:

DATE:

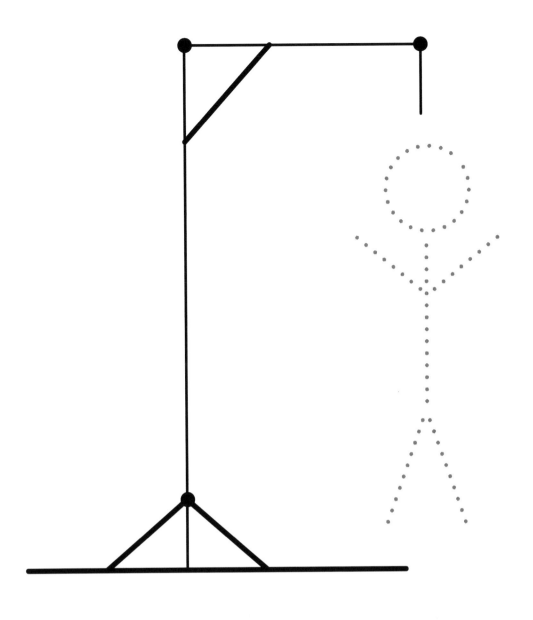

A B C D E F G H I J K L M N
O P Q R S T U V W X Y Z

PLAYED BY:

DATE:

COOKOUT

COLORED BY:

DATE:

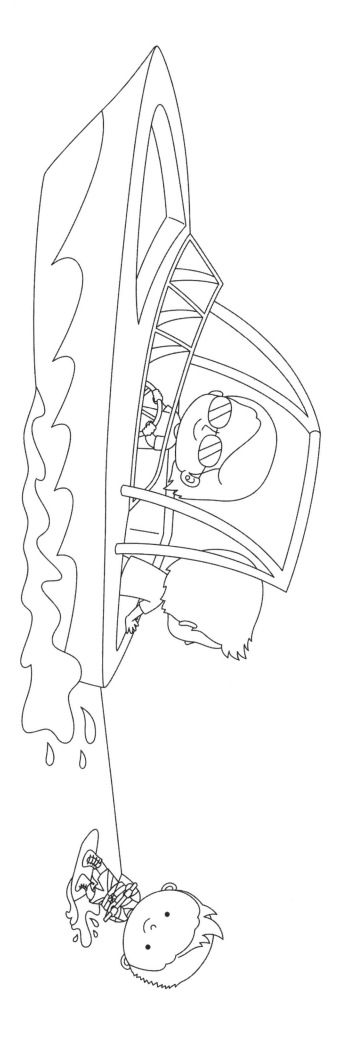

WAKEBOARDING

COLORED BY:

DATE:

FIREWORKS
ON THE
FOURTH!

COLORED BY:

DATE:

MY CLEAR LAKE MEMORIES

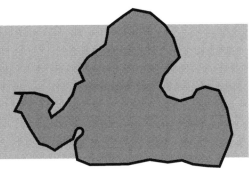

WRITTEN BY:

DATE:

FIREWORKS
ON THE
FOURTH!

COLORED BY:

DATE:

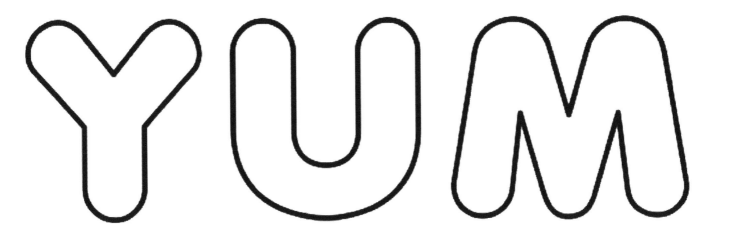

COLORED BY:

DATE:

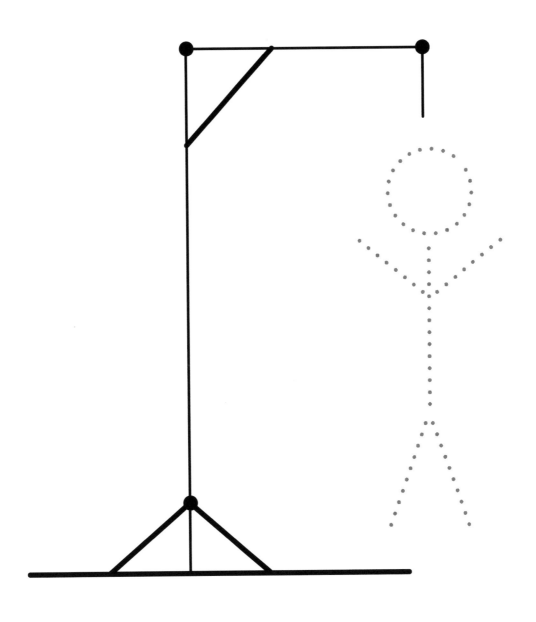

A B C D E F G H I J K L M N
O P Q R S T U V W X Y Z

PLAYED BY:

DATE:

FISHING

WORM

COLORED BY:

DATE:

BONFIRE

COLORED BY:

DATE:

COLORED BY:

DATE:

COLORED BY:

DATE:

COLORED BY:

DATE:

FILL IN THE BLANK SILLY STORY

A RAINY DAY AT CLEAR LAKE

It's fun being at Clear Lake, even when it's a rainy

day! It was raining so hard that it sounded like

_____ were hitting the roof! The
plural noun

temperature outside was _____ degrees. So,
number

we put on our _____ and decided to
article of clothing

bake _____. The recipe called for
food

_____, _____, and _____.
food   food   food

It said to then stir them together for

_____ minutes and bake it at
number

_____ degrees. While they were in the
number

oven, we decided to color. We used a _____
color

crayon and colored _____ with it.
place

COLORED BY:

DATE:

DRAW A PICTURE OF YOUR FAVORITE SNACK TO EAT AT CLEAR LAKE

I'M HERE FOR THE Snacks

DRAWN BY:

DATE:

PLAYED BY:

DATE:

FISHING

COLORED BY:

DATE:

FILL IN THE BLANK SILLY STORY

RIDING MY WAVERUNNER

It was a _____ day on Clear Lake, and I

adjective

decided to take my waverunner out on the lake. I had

just filled the tank up with _____ and I

liquid

knew it would be good for at least _____

number

hours on the water. My waverunner is

_____ and _____ and I

color   color

bought it at _____.

store

When I got out to the middle of the lake I saw bigger

waves than I'd ever seen before. They were as big as

_____. It was a thrill to ride over the

plural noun

waves at the speed of _____ mph. What a

number

_____ day of riding my waverunner!

adjective

COLORED BY:

DATE:

COLORED BY:

DATE:

SAILBOAT RACES!

COLORED BY:

DATE:

COLORED BY:

DATE:

FILL IN THE BLANK SILLY STORY

FISHING AT CLEAR LAKE

It was early one _____ morning, and I

day of the week

filled my thermos with _____ and

liquid

headed out onto Clear Lake to fish. I baited my hook

with _____ and cast it into the water.

type of food

Suddenly, I felt a _____ nibble and

adjective

I began to reel in my line. _____, I had

exclamatory term

caught a/an _____

adjective

_____! After a struggle, I finally

noun

got it into the boat and off the hook. It weighed

_____ pounds! I am so excited to hang it

number

on my _____ wall! What a

room in the house

_____ day of fishing!

adjective

COLORED BY:

DATE:

Tic Tac Turtle

PLAYED BY:

DATE:

COLORED BY:

DATE:

FLOAT

COLORED BY:

DATE:

SUNSCREEN

COLORED BY:

DATE:

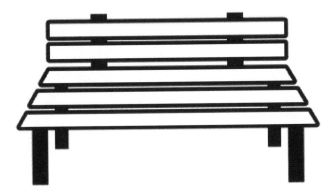

COLORED BY:

DATE:

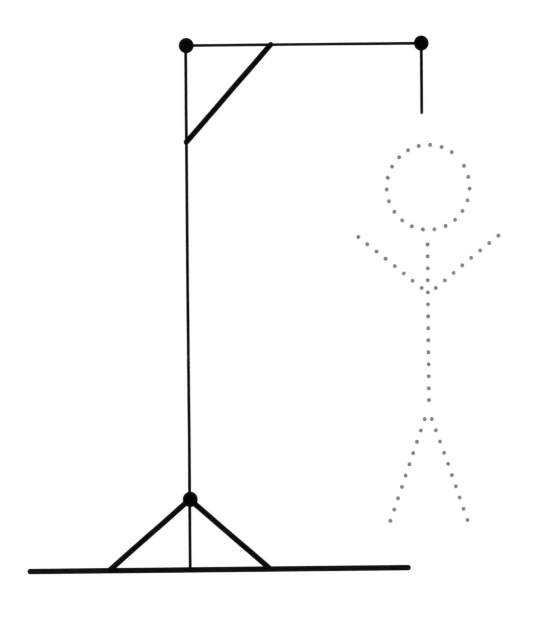

A B C D E F G H I J K L M N
O P Q R S T U V W X Y Z

PLAYED BY:

DATE:

TREATS

COLORED BY:

DATE:

FILL IN THE BLANK SILLY STORY

BOATING ON CLEAR LAKE

We love taking pontoon rides on Clear Lake! We go

out every day at _____. We like to pack
                        time

snacks to eat on the pontoon. Our favorite snacks

are _____ and _____. Usually,
        food   food

_____ drives the pontoon at a speed of

name of family member

_____ mph. The rest of us on the boat
        number

like to _____. Sometimes we sing
            verb

songs. Our favorite songs are _____
                                name of song

and _____. It's so
        name of song

_____ to go on pontoon rides on
        adjective

Clear Lake!

COLORED BY:

DATE:

PIZZA

COLORED BY:

DATE:

BUBBLES

COLORED BY:

DATE:

COLORED BY:

DATE:

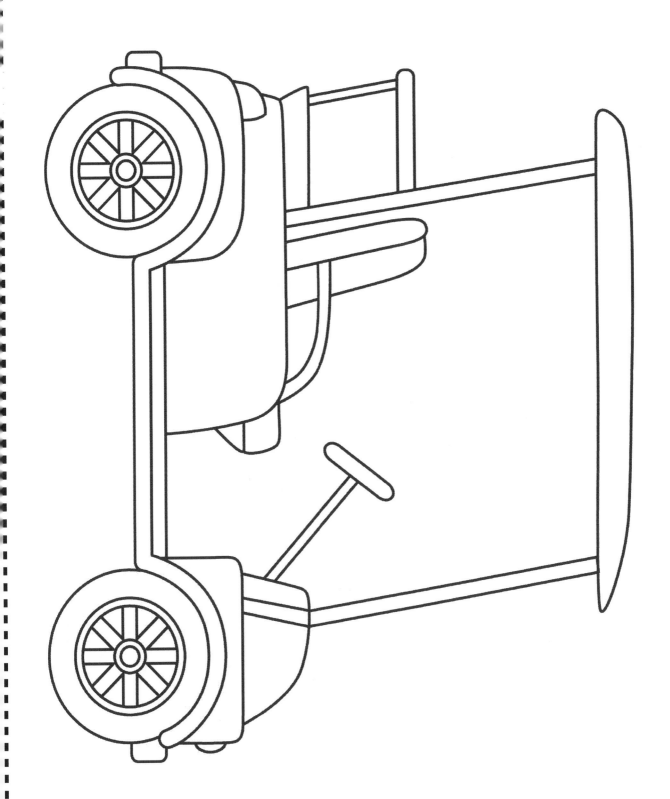

PLAYED BY:

DATE:

COLORED BY:

DATE:

FILL IN THE BLANK SILLY STORY

PADDLE BOARDING ADVENTURES

Early one morning, I decided to go paddle boarding

with my friend _____. We own
                   friend's name

_____ paddle boards, and they are
      number

_____ feet long. We decided to head toward
     number

_____'s house on our paddle boards.
      friend's name

It took us _____ minutes to get there. We
               number

were pretty tired, and our _____ were
                              body part plural

sore. One the way back home, we passed an

_____ floating in the lake. It was
      animal

such a _____ day of paddle boarding!
           adjective

PLAYED BY:

DATE:

COLORED BY:

DATE:

COLORED BY:

DATE:

KAYAK

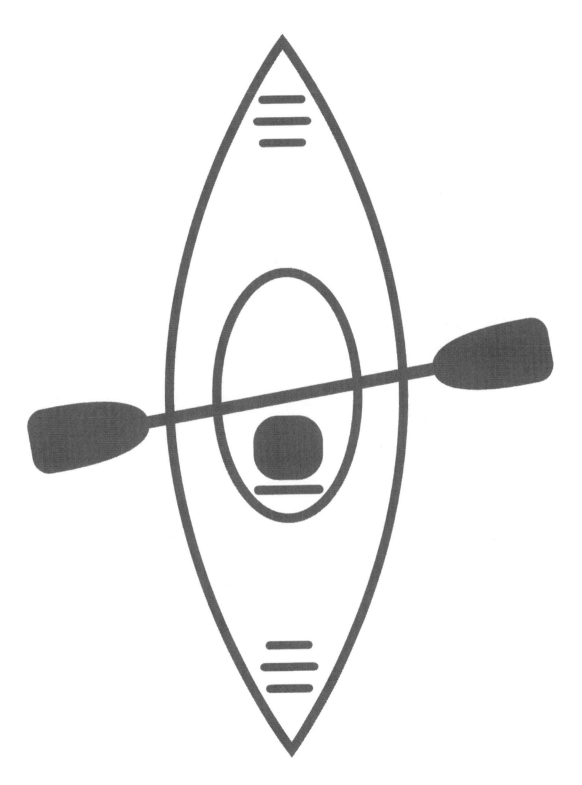

COLORED BY:

DATE:

BOAT PARADE

COLORED BY:

DATE:

COLORED BY:

DATE:

DONUTS

COLORED BY:

DATE:

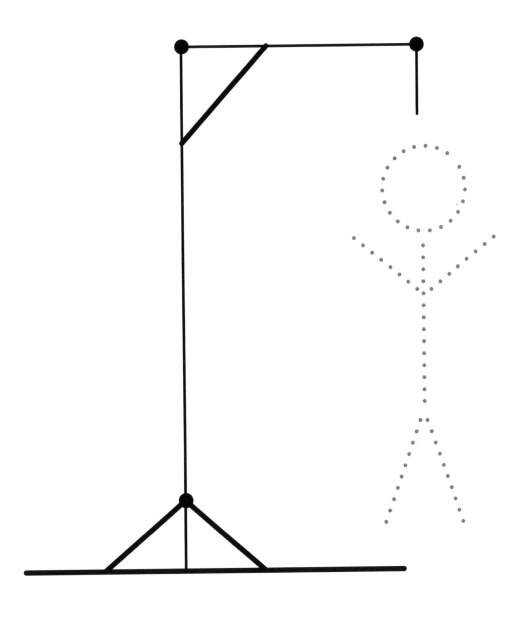

A B C D E F G H I J K L M N
O P Q R S T U V W X Y Z

PLAYED BY:

DATE:

WAVERUNNER

COLORED BY:

DATE:

Tic Tac Turtle

PLAYED BY:

DATE:

BOAT

PARADE

COLORED BY:

DATE:

COLORED BY:

DATE:

MY CLEAR LAKE MEMORIES

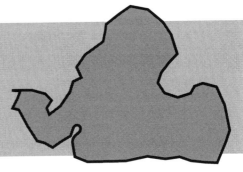

WRITTEN BY:

DATE:

BIKE RIDES

COLORED BY:

DATE:

SKI

COLORED BY:

DATE:

BOAT PARADE

COLORED BY:

DATE:

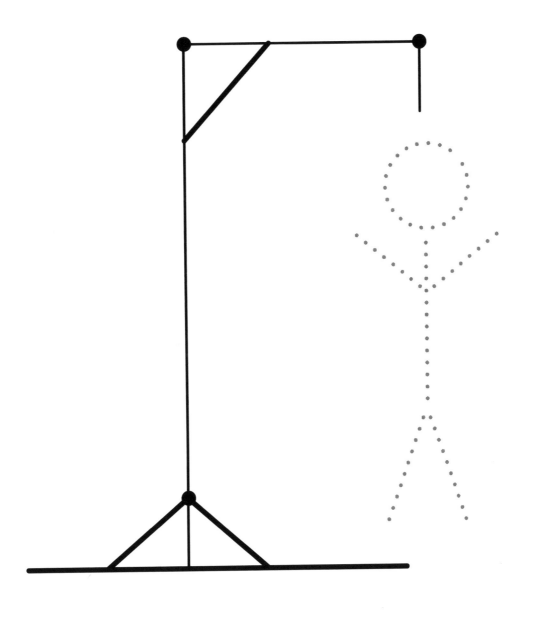

A B C D E F G H I J K L M N
O P Q R S T U V W X Y Z

PLAYED BY:

DATE:

DONUTS

COLORED BY:

DATE:

HAMILTON LAKE

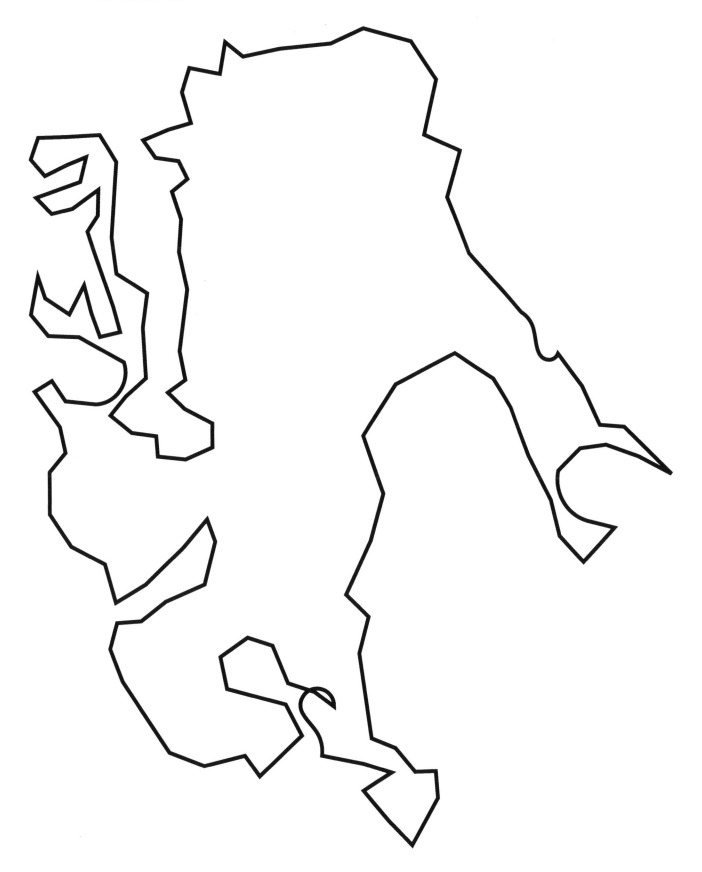

COLORED BY:

DATE:

Tic Tac Turtle

PLAYED BY:

DATE:

FOUR BUOYS IN A ROW

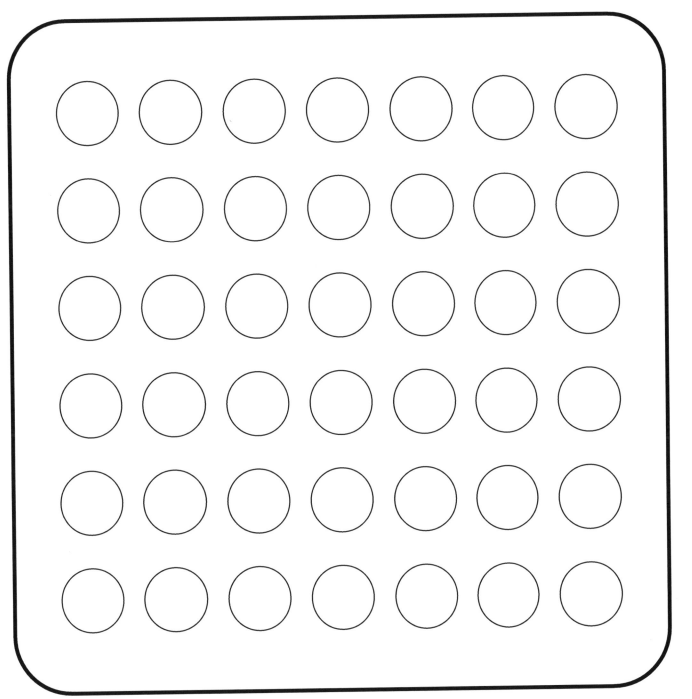

TAKE TURNS COLORING IN THE BUOYS AND
SEE WHO CAN GET FOUR IN A ROW FIRST!
(VERTICAL, HORIZONTAL, OR DIAGONAL)

PLAYED BY:

DATE:

COLORED BY:

DATE:

COLORED BY:

DATE:

DRAW A PICTURE OF YOUR FAVORITE SNACK TO EAT AT CLEAR LAKE

DRAWN BY:

DATE:

FOUR BUOYS IN A ROW

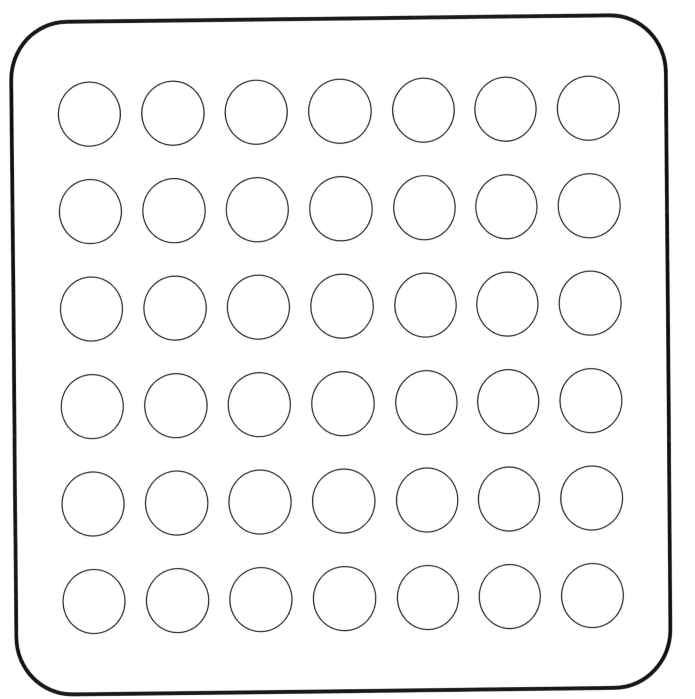

TAKE TURNS COLORING IN THE BUOYS AND SEE WHO CAN GET FOUR IN A ROW FIRST! (VERTICAL, HORIZONTAL, OR DIAGONAL)

PLAYED BY:

DATE:

MY CLEAR LAKE MEMORIES

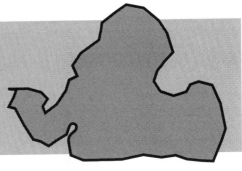

WRITTEN BY:

DATE:

CHECK OUT **ALL** OF OUR NORTHERN INDIANA/SOUTHERN MICHIGAN LAKE BOOKS!

BASS AND PIKE PRESS

INCLUDING...

LAKE JAMES
JIMMERSON LAKE
SNOW LAKE
CROOKED LAKE
COLDWATER LAKE
LAKE GAGE & LIME LAKE
LAKE GEORGE
CLEAR LAKE
LAKE PLEASANT
HAMILTON LAKE

AVAILABLE ON AMAZON

AVAILABLE ON AMAZON

AND LOOK FOR OUR
AT THE LAKE
SERIES COLORING BOOKS!

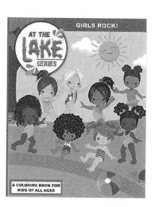

BASS AND
PIKE PRESS

Made in the USA
Columbia, SC
11 August 2020